# How to res╌ ╌╌╌
# CHILDHOODS
### spent in former
# CHILDREN'S HOMES,
### orphanages, cottage homes
### and other children's institutions

---

## Gudrun Jane Limbrick

ISBN 978-1-903210-29-1



WordWorks
enquiries@wordworks.org.uk
www.wordworks.org.uk

# Contents

# Introduction

Many many thousands of people spent time as children in some sort of residential home or institution. Whether their stay in the home was for their whole childhoods or just for a few weeks, the experience can have a profound impact on the not only their childhoods but throughout their lives.

Unfortunately, it can be extremely difficult to find out time spent in a children's home. As the founder of the Former Children's Homes website, I get many enquiries from people who have discovered an ancestor was in a particular home and are looking to find out more about what life might have been like for them and why they were in care in the first place.

This guide has been written to help these people in their search for information. It offers no guarantees - sometimes, no matter how thoroughly you search, there is no information to be found. But the five step process will help you on a logical course to ensure that you try everything possible and explain your what your rights are in terms of accessing what you have found.

I wish you the best of luck with your search.

Gudrun Limbrick BA Hons Oxon MA
www.formerchildrenshomes.org.uk

Former Children's Homes
www.formerchildrenshomes.org.uk

# The need for children's homes

It is probably true to say that the need for large numbers of children to be looked after outside the family started to happen because of industrialisation and urbanisation in the eighteenth and nineteenth centuries.

Before we started living in towns and cities, children tended to be looked after by the wider family if the immediate family could not take care of them. Thus, for example, if a child's parents were ill or died, the children would simply be taken under the wings of other family members who lived in the same village.

Where this was not possible, the local church may have stepped in to support the child. This support was formalised through the Poor Relief Act of 1601. Local people paid a tax to the church which the church then gave out as Poor Relief (a small amount of money) to the destitute members of the local community.

However, industrialisation in the nineteenth century meant that people moved away from their local parishes, their wider families, and into our rapidly growing towns and cities. When people could not work, for whatever reason, they needed support that was no longer available from the wider family or local community. A new way of looking after

*George Cruikshank's illustration of Charles Dickens' Oliver Twist asking for me watched, the horror showing on the faces of the other children in the workhouse*

our poor, disabled, or sick adults and children was needed.

The workhouse was provided as the main solution. These were vast buildings in which people could be housed in return for hard, manual work. There were no home comforts and life in the workhouse was hard. The workhouse was not meant to be inviting. People in need voluntarily entered the workhouse only as a last resort when they had no other means to support themselves and their families.

While adults entered the workhouse of their own volition, children living on the streets would often be picked up and placed there with no element of choice. Charles Dickens, writing *Oliver Twist,* described how Oliver, just a young boy, went to the workhouse and cried himself to sleep on a hard bed, had too little to eat, and spent his days pulling apart strands of old rope - a task known as picking oakum. Workhouse life, even for children, was undoubtedly hard.

Not everyone, however, thought that the workhouse was the best solution for children. Some enterprising philanthropists noticed the plight of street

*Youngsters in Crumpsall Workhouse in 1895*

children and established orphanages and ragged schools for them. Thomas Coram built his 'hospital' for foundlings in London in 1739 Dr Barnardo, also in London, set up his first ragged school in 1867 - the first of 95 children's homes he established during his lifetime.

Many other philanthropists set up orphanages in other towns and cities - Josiah Mason, the pen manufacturer, in Birmingham, the Crossley brothers in Halifax and George Muller in Bristol for example.

Local churches and religious organisations were also setting up orphanages, often run by nuns. In this way, the Victorian era saw a massive surge in provision for children in need outside the workhouse.

The local authorities - in the form of the Guardians of the Poor who had responsibility for social welfare in their locality - were also setting up children's homes, and whole complexes of children's homes known as cottage homes from the late nineteenth century. At first these were linked to the workhouses, later they became institutions independent of the workhouse.

In those early years of the first orphanages, many children were indeed orphans or had been abandoned by their families because they could not afford to look after them. Many were living on the street, begging or thieving to survive before being taken into the orphanages.

As the decades passed, however, the proportion of children in care who were actually orphans diminished and children were taken in for a variety of other reasons. Some of the very wide range of reasons I have come across in my research are as follows:

- The death of one or both parents
- The illness or disability of one of both parents
- The death or injury of the father in the armed services
- One or both parents go into prison
- Unemployment of the family bread-winner

- Parents enter the workhouse

- Mother is about to give birth

- Child's illness or disability

- Child is thought likely to commit a crime

- Breakdown of the parents' marriage*

- Child is convicted of a crime*

- Truancy*

- Abuse or risk of abuse of the child*

*These reasons appear more common than the others after the Second World War.*

These days, the media often concerns itself with children forcibly taken from their families by the authorities because of concerns about their welfare or because a crime had been committed. In the early days of residential childcare, children were more often voluntarily placed in an orphanage simply because a family couldn't afford to feed them either because of a family tragedy or a lack of work. This very much follows on from the workhouse ethos in which people 'voluntarily' placed themselves in the dreaded workhouse when they had run out of all other options. The welfare state, of course, did not exist to support families until after the Second World War.

*A young child learning a trade in the first NCH home in Bonner Road, London (1889)*

One of the main aims of the early children's homes and orphanages was to equip the children with some way of making their living in later years. Boys received what was known as 'industrial training', some form of practical training in trades such as carpentry, shoe-making and

*Exercise drill for the boys at Stockwell Orphanage*

such like. Some children's homes had land so the children would learn farming skills.

Domestic skills were taught to the girls with a view to them going into domestic service. Many domestic service jobs of the time were live-in thereby giving the girls accommodation as well as a means of earning a wage.

Boys often went into apprenticeships and many joined the armed services which again, afforded them a roof over their heads, very important when a young person did not have a family to live with.

After education was made compulsory in the 1880 Education Act, education for education's sake became more important than this vocational training. Most children's homes at the turn of the nineteenth century had small schools or school rooms as part of their fabric.

A second important element was healthcare. Children on the street or living with very poor families would not have had access to healthcare. Some children's homes were established specifically with healthcare in mind - such as the convalescent homes and open air schools. Others had healthcare for the children as an intrinsic part of what was available. Many of the cottage homes complexes, for example, had their own infirmaries staffed by nurses and visited by a local doctor. Orphanages also had provision for looking after children's health - Mason's Orphanage, for example had two homeopathic doctors.

It was not unusual for children's homes to be isolated from the rest of the community when there was a bout of infectious illness, such as scarlet fever or tuberculosis (also known as consumption or TB), amongst the children. Visiting would be curtailed (if it were allowed at all) and children would be kept from going to the local schools. Other children's homes, going along with the popular idea that fresh air was the best thing for any ailing child, had rooms which opened out to the gardens and grounds to act as convalescent wards.

In this manner, children who were from very poor and disadvantaged backgrounds were given shelter, education/training and healthcare by the early children's homes. Since the Second World War there have been many changes. Most children are now fostered or adopted rather than placed in children's homes.

Those homes that do still exist are much smaller and run by professional, qualified residential care staff. The old, large institutions have gone, mostly demolished.

*The infirmary, Aston Union Cottage Homes*

# Types of children's home

Throughout this book, I use the shorthand 'children's home' to describe what is, in reality, a wide range of different types of institution. These institutions had two things in common - firstly they were residential, and secondly, they took in children. Aside from these basic linking factors, the situations of the children they took in and the types of care they offered often differed significantly from one to the other. Although the different terms have been different ways over the decades, here I give a rough glossary of what the different types of home are:

## Children's homes

As a term, 'children's home' did not really gain popularity until after the Second World War. We now use it to mean all sorts of types of residential home for children. Before the Second World War, it was much more common to divide children's homes into different types. In the 1970s, some children's homes became known as 'community homes'.

*The Lamorbey Cottage Homes— cottage homes were often gated*

*A huge orphanage building in Snaresbrook, London in the early 1900s*

## Cottage Homes

These were built towards the end of the nineteenth century, usually by the Poor Law Union - the local public sector organisation responsible for social welfare and the forerunner of the modern local council system. Cottage Homes were built as alternative accommodation for children from the workhouses. They were commonly (although not always) built as a small, self-contained village with a number of houses for the children (perhaps ten to thirty children in each with a live-in house mother) and had, on site, amenities such as chapel, school, workshops for training, hospital, sports facilities etc. Not all Unions built cottage homes in the village style. In the same time period, some chose instead to build (or use) just one or two cottages, perhaps on an ordinary street. Known as scattered homes, these housed between thirty and sixty children under the care of a live-in foster mother.

## Orphanages

The 'hey day' of the orphanage was in the nineteenth century when they were established by philanthropists, churches and charities for children who had lost both their parents. Being in an orphanage does not, however, exclude those children who had one or more parents as admission policies changed and relaxed over the years. Orphanages were typically large, mixed gender institutions.

### Remand homes

A remand home differs from most orphanages or children's homes in that the child or young person would have been sent there by the court having been found guilty of an offence. A borstal was another type of detention centre, run by the Prison Service, and abolished in 1982.

### Reformatories / Reform schools

The reformatories were, in essence, the forerunners of the remand homes and youth detention centres. Children were sent to the Reformatories by the courts when they had been found guilty of a crime. They were, in essence, a child's version of a prison with strict regimes and few freedoms.

### Ragged schools / Industrial schools

Another development of the nineteenth century was the industrial school (initially often known as ragged schools). Whereas those sent to the reform schools by the courts had been found guilty of a crime, those sent to the

industrial schools were destitute or were thought, because of their circumstances or temperament, to be likely to commit a crime in the future.

### Approved schools

The industrial schools were strict like the reform schools and the differences between reform schools and industrial schools gradually disappeared until, in 1933, both were renamed approved schools.

*A house in Portsmouth which was thought to be the first ragged school, set up by John Pound in 1818*

## Working boys' homes / hostels

These hostels were built for older boys, perhaps who had left the cottage homes. The idea was that they would be helped to get work and, once in employment, they would pay their wages to the hostel which would provide board and lodgings in return. The hostels acted as a sort of halfway house between residential care and independent living.

## Service girls home

This was the girls' version of the working boys' hostel. While the boys would often be encouraged to take up apprenticeships in manual trades, the girls would be encouraged to go into domestic service. Often, they would find a domestic service role which was live-in.

## Emigration homes

These were homes set up with the sole purpose of emigrating children to the New World - Canada and Australia primarily. This was thought to achieve the two aims of giving a new start to destitute or orphaned children and providing good labour for the New World. Some emigration homes had the added aim of spreading religion in the New World by sending out Christian children.

*Fairbridge Farm School, Pinjarra, Western Australia. This children's home was set up to take in children emigrated from children's homes in England*

It is not only dedicated emigration homes, however, that emigrated children. Other homes and organisations also sent children overseas including, for example, Barnardo's and the National Children's Home, although they may have used the services of an emigration home for to conduct the emigration. Emigrating children was at a peak in the Victorian era, gradually declined towards the approach of the World Wars and was finally halted by the 1948 Children Act.

**Convalescent Homes**

St Mary's Convalescent Home for Children, Broadstairs

Convalescent homes were rarely a permanent home for children. Instead they were places where children were sent (either from their family home or a children's home) to recuperate from an illness. One of the most common illnesses requiring a spell in the convalescent home was tuberculosis (also known as TB or consumption). It was thought that fresh air was the key to recovery and so convalescent homes were often by the sea or in the countryside. These were generally independently run.

**Mother and baby homes**

These were not children's homes as such as they took in pregnant women, generally unmarried, who stayed there until they gave birth. At this point, or soon after, the baby would be 'removed' for adoption. This was thought to be the way to deal with the perceived shame of having babies outside of marriage. The mothers-to-be may have gone into the homes voluntarily but may also have been forced in due to family / society pressures. There were many types of such home, some were small private homes, others large institutions, perhaps the most famous being the Magdalen Laundries of Ireland. In England, the workhouse was also commonly used as a place where a woman would go to have her baby when no other options were available. The baby may then have gone into the cottage homes. In the UK, these were generally privately run.

**Open Air Schools**

The first open air schools in England started in the early 1900s. Largely for children with tuberculosis, they were designed to give children fresh air to aid their recovery. Thus, whole walls would be missing leaving children to study in the open air. Some lessons would be held outside and it wasn't unusual for bedrooms to be open to the elements. Some open air schools were for children to come just on school days, others were residential. When tuberculosis became less common after the Second World War, the open air

*Oak Bank Open Air School: nap-time in the open air*

schools gradually took in other children who were thought to be 'delicate' and in need of fresh air and exercise, including children with disabilities.

## Hospitals

To add to our confusion, some early children's homes were called 'hospitals' rather than homes. If you do find a reference to a child in a hospital in the eighteenth century, it can take some detective work to establish that it actually was a residential institution rather a medical hospital in the sense that we would understand it today. Arguably the most famous of this type of hospital is the London Foundling Hospital. This was set up by a sea captain, Thomas Coram, in 1741 for the "education and maintenance of exposed and deserted young children".

*The Foundling Hospital moved to Berkhamstead in 1935*

## Receiving Homes

Receiving homes were established to take in children temporarily before a permanent placement was arranged for them. In the early twentieth century, the routine was to give children coming into the receiving home a bath and de-louse them, no doubt a very unpleasant experience. Receiving homes were also sometimes called probation homes. In the second half of the twentieth century, they were more usually called reception centres. Most receiving homes were run by the local authority with just one in any locality.

# Looking for records

Looking for records of children's homes is not an easy process. There is no central information point, no central deposit of records, no database, and no single agency that has responsibility for helping you through the process. There is very little computerisation and there are no standard guidelines that archives use to determine which records can be made available to the public.

To further complicate matters, we are often chasing records for children's homes which closed perhaps a century before and which were run by a small committee, which has long-since disappeared, and not a local authority.

However, finding records can bring a wealth of understanding about the childhoods of the individuals we are researching and so is worth the search.

The following pages will take you, step-by-step, through the process of looking for records. While following the steps is by no means a guarantee of finding anything at all, if you take each step in turn, you reduce the risk of missing something key out.

**Looking for your own records?**

The process for looking for your own records can differ significantly than that for records relating to someone else.

**Please skip straight to page 53.**

| Step 1 | The basics |
| Step 2 | What to look for |
| Step 3 | Where to look |
| Step 4 | Know your rights |
| Step 5 | Find and creating unofficial records |

# Step 1

# THE BASICS

As a family historian, it is likely that you will have come to this point via one of two routes:

i.      You have discovered , through census or other records, an ancestor who, as a child, spent time in a residential institution, or

ii      A relative has told you about their own time, or the time of another relative, in a children's home.

In the latter case, you may have the opportunity to ask some questions about the individual and the institution if your relative is still living and willing to talk about it. If this is the case, find out what you can and record the answers or write them down. First-hand information about some of these institutions is a rare and valuable thing (see page 50).

In the former case, you will have some basic details such as the approximate date of birth of the individual, the child's name and the name and location of the institution from the census return itself.

In either case, the first step is to arm yourself with some basic information. This will not only add to your understanding but will also help pinpoint the individual when it comes to looking for records.

1.      Find an exact date of birth. This will enable records, should they exist, to be located. Services such as freebmd.org.uk will tell you when a birth was registered, the birth certificate will give a precise date of birth as well as the names of known parents. Important clues, such as the absence of a father on a birth certificate, as to the circumstances of the family my also be found.

2.      Find out what you can about the parent / parents. The names of the parent/s can be found on the child's birth certificate. The parental death certificate may, for example, may reveal that one or both parents died in the time preceding the child being at the children's

home and thus may be an indication as to why the child was there.

3    Find out what you can about the institution. The two best websites for this are www.formerchildrenshomes.org.uk which includes details of a range of children's homes, orphanages, cottage homes etc. and www.workhouses.org which has details of cottage homes run by the Guardians of the Poor. This is a key bit of research as it will give you the locality of the institution and any alternative names. Children's homes had a habit of changing names. Pinning these down can aid your later research enormously.

A great source of information on this can be **Kelly's Directory** if you can find the one/s relating to the approximate time and locality of the home you are looking for. These trade directories were published from the mid 1800s and are often found in libraries. They frequently list charities, schools, homes and orphanages and so may give you a name and an address and other details such as the names of key staff members.

**ORDERING CERTIFICATES**

To get a birth certificate, you will need the name (at birth, not a married name), the approximate date of birth and the place of birth. This information can be found on census records. You can get the index number of the birth (the GRO Index), from **freebmd.org.uk** and this may speed up the process. Either order online at **www.gro.gov.uk** or contact the Registry Office in the location of the birth. The process for marriage and death certificates is the same—although you will need the married name for death certificates. You will need to approach the registry office in the location of the marriage or death.

# Step 2

# WHAT TO LOOK FOR

## Official records about children's homes

Records about children's homes are sadly in short supply. Many children's homes have gone undocumented and it is a struggle to find either details about the history of the homes or information about individuals who lived there.

Where official information does exist, it can be divided into two different types:

*Information about individuals* Primarily, these records include case files and admission/discharge registers. Because these contain very personal information about individuals and their families, there are generally very strict restrictions on who can have access to these documents.

*Information about homes* Primarily, these records include annual reports, minutes from committees and correspondence but they may include other details about the finances and practical details of running the home.

There is, of course, no guarantee that either type of information will exist (or did ever exist) for any specific home, or for any specific individual in that home.

### What do official records look like?

Whoever ran the children's home we are looking at, the same sort of official records might exist:

### Case files

The first records I will look at are the case files. These were, until the advent of computers and digital record-keeping, stacks of papers (such as letters, forms, reports, memos and other such items) which were drawn up and kept by social workers, in the main, about a particular child or family. These can contain all sorts of useful information about a person detailing why they went into care, what happened to them when they were there, medical reports, and may include details about the family and home life and perhaps even a photograph. Because these documents are such personal data sources, they are of concern only to those looking for their own records rather than family historians who will be seeking older documentation such as registers.

## Registers

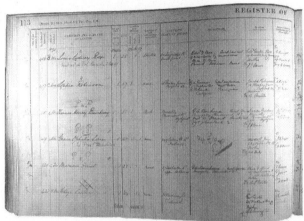

Many institutions, pre–Second World War institutions particularly (although not exclusively), kept registers which listed all the children who moved into the home. These registers are large handwritten books which can contain surprisingly useful information.

Commonly, registers gave the full name of the child, the date they went into the home, the date they left and the date of birth. They might also record who the next of kin was and their address. This might not sound like a lot of information but it might be all that exists in many cases or all that is available. I have known cases where these snippets have enabled someone to trace a entire family or piece together a whole history which was just a blank..

One of the problems of accessing the information in the registers is that, because they contain private information about many individuals, they may not be made available to the public. The other problem is that they are handwritten, often in writing that is difficult to read, and not in a useful order (ie. alphabetical) but in order of the date of admission - generally a date we don't know. Through years of use, these registers can also be very worn and fragile documents.

Registers might relate to a single home, or might relate to a whole organisation or local authority and thus might incorporate information about many different children's homes. The latter is a great boon in those instances where you know a person was in care in a particular area but you don't know which home or homes they may have been in.

People are often surprised to find that the case files or registers relating a person's time in care no longer exists. There was no legal obligation for a local authority to keep case files and other records of this nature once the person in question had reached the age of 21. Some authorities destroyed all files, some did not. In other cases, files and other records have been destroyed by other means. For example, records relating to the time before the Second World War in Portsmouth were destroyed by bombing.

**Committee minutes and other official papers**

Every children's home is run by someone. The decisions affecting the home are usually decided by a board - whether it is a group of councillors in the local authority; managers in Social Services; the board of a charity, the board of the Guardians of the Poor.

These minutes, if they have been kept, can potentially give information about individual children who were in the homes at any one time. These minutes do, of course, contain much confidential information and so it is unlikely that they could be made public as a matter of course unless significant time has lapsed.

Other official records of this type may include:

*Punishment books*—listing children who had been punished and the nature of the punishment

*Visitors' books*—a book detailing all the visitors to the children's home

*Stores records* - what supplies were brought into the home for staff and children.

There were no guidelines about what records children's homes should keep at any one time so some kept more records than others of the nature above. There were also no guidelines as to what records should be stored and archived, thus not all will have survived even if they were kept at the time.

**Annual reports**

The beauty of the annual report is that they were written to be made public and thus they are very different to the other official records I have mentioned so far. Like the other official records, however, if we are lucky they can contain some very interesting information and sometimes some personal details.

Typically the annual report will give interesting data like the numbers of children who were admitted in that financial year, the financial statement including the costs of accommodating the children and where the funding came from. Often, they will include details of particular children who are new or have achieved something of note.

Interesting accounts of what day-to-day life is like in the institution and plans for future development may also be included.

Not all institutions, by any means, produced annual reports but both institutions run by the Guardians of the Poor and private institutions were equally as likely, or as unlikely, to produce annual reports. Finding them, however, is another matter. Try the libraries and archives closest to the location of the institution. Sadly not all institutions published annual reports, and not all annual reports have survived the passage of time.

An important consideration is that annual reports are often written for a very particular reason—to please existing funders and encourage new ones—and thus the writers may tend to write particularly glowing accounts of achievements and their successes with children, perhaps brushing over some of the more negative aspects. Whenever you are reading a published document about a home, it is important to consider who was publishing it and why before you decide how much credence to give to the contents.

**Other official documents to explore**

Your local archivist should also be able to advise you on whether there are other sets of official records which might help in your own particular search such as:

*Court records* - these can be useful if a child was sent to an institution, such as a remand home or reform school by the courts because they had committed a crime.

*School records* - for some schools, records survive and they may give some information about the person you are seeking.

*Hospital records* - again, some hospital records might exist. Many institutions had their own medical facilities but for particular illnesses and operations, some children may have been sent out to local hospitals. The details in the records, however, are likely to be primarily medical and thus of limited value for researching what a childhood was like.

*Adoption records* - adoption and fostering (or boarding out as it was known) records can indicate what happened to a child after they left a children's home or, on occasion, some children were boarded out and then returned to the children's home when the boarding out arrangement did not work out.

All of these records listed can, of course, contain very sensitive personal information and thus the archives holding them may have strict limitations in place on who can look at the records.

# Using an archive - checklist

| | |
|---|---|
| ○ | Most archives, private and local authority will want you bring some form of ID before they can show you some documents. Check with them before you set off. |
| ○ | If you are looking for records of a relative which are not public, you may need to take proof of their death. |
| ○ | Most archives will charge a fee for any research they need to do on your behalf. This is generally charged by the hour. Make sure you know what you are committing to in advance and set a limit on how much you want to spend. |
| ○ | Personal documents about individuals are usually 'closed' under the Data Protection Act and thus a member of the public cannot view them without special permission. The Act was not really designed for care records and archives have to interpret the Act as best they can. Don't expect one archive to behave exactly like another in terms of the access you might get. Ask before you go. |
| ○ | Archivists are generally very happy to chat about what you will be able to have access to. It is worth talking through with them what you are looking for in advance to save you a wasted journey. They may also have specialist knowledge on your area of research which can be extremely helpful. |
| ○ | Many larger archives are going through the process of putting details about the records they hold online. You can then look through what you might be interested in from the comfort of your own computer. Note down the reference number and the name of any document you are interested in as they will help the archivist enormously on the day of your visit and save you some time. |
| ○ | As well as copious notepaper and a pencil (some archives will not permit the use of ballpoint or ink pens), take a camera. Some documents can be photographed (check first!) which will save you a lot of time in taking notes. |

# Step 3

# WHERE TO LOOK

---

*Who ran the children's home?*

The question of who ran a children's home might not have been important to the children who lived there and it may not mean much to us now. However, finding out who or what ran a particular institution can be key in finding out where the records of those homes now lie.

However, a word of warning, finding out what body ran a particular home does not necessarily determine how easy it might be to access the records of a person's time there, but it is at least a starting point.

Similarly, finding out what sort of body ran a home will not necessarily tell you anything about the quality of care the home provided and the sort of lives the children there experienced.

An internet search (try **www.formerchildrenshomes.org.uk** in the first instance) may tell you who ran the home. Failing that, contact the library or public archives local to where the home was based.

The **National Archives** can also be an informative first port of call. If they hold information themselves, they often include a potted history of the institution. Find their contact details on page 58.

## LOCAL AUTHORITY

*Downend Cottage Homes, Bristol, was run by the Guardians of the Poor*

The biggest manager of children's homes in the UK is the public sector. Most children's homes and other institutions have been managed by the local authority. This is simply because running a large institution is expensive and local authorities have been able to raise this scale of funding through rates and taxes whereas other bodies might struggle.

*Homes run by the Poor Law Union / the Guardians of the Poor*

The Poor Law Unions, in place from 1834 to 1930, were effectively the forerunner of the local authority social services. Each area had a Poor Law Union which was run by a Board of individuals called the Guardians of the Poor. Significantly, it was the Guardians of The Poor who ran the workhouses, and any children's institutions associated with the workhouses. In 1930, the work of the Guardians was taken over by the local council structure that we still have today. There is a good chance that an institution for poor children between 1834 and 1930 would have been run by the Guardians of the Poor and that this institution would have passed to the local council in 1930.

Homes run by the local authority after the 1930s are likely to have been run by the education department, the children's department (after 1948), or social services (after 1970) all of which come under the auspices of the city, borough or county council.

### Records

Generally, any surviving records are held by the official local authority council archives. In the first instance, contact the archives, records office or the main library in the locality of the children's home in question.

Significantly, before 1991 local authorities did not have a legal obligation to keep records after the individual in care had turned 21. In 1991, the law changed meaning that records created after 1991 must be retained for 75 years after the 18th birthday of the individual in question.

In practice, things were changing before the law changed. The 1980s, in many local authorities, has tended to be the point at which records were kept rather than destroyed. It was earlier in other local authorities.

What this lack of legal obligation to keep local authority records means in practice is that record-archiving has been patchy. Some local authorities have kept more than others, and different eras may have more complete records than others.

Another significant feature of records held by local authorities is that they are subject the Freedom of Information Act and individuals can apply to see some information through this Act. More on this later on page 44.

*Athelstan House Remand Home, Birmingham, was set up in 1911 by members of the Cadbury family and run as an independent institution. However, it was taken over by the Council in 1930. All surviving records are in the local authority archive*

## PHILANTHROPISTS

In the Victorian era, the need to help poor or abandoned children who were seen on the streets of our newly growing towns and cities was clear to see. This was an era in which many philanthropists took up the challenge of caring for these children. Some self-made men funded the building and running of large orphanages such as the Crossley brothers in Halifax.

### Records

The orphanages founded by individual philanthropists have long since gone. Sadly, in many cases, their records have long since gone as well as there was no legal imperative and no process in place for preserving records. Places to try:

i. The first port of call is to find out which local authority covers the area in which the orphanage was located and go to the local public archives / library. They may either hold any existing records themselves or be able to tell you where you might look.

ii. There may also be an old boys'/girls' association who may hold records in their own archives or be experienced helping people to locate them. You may find the association through an internet search or by asking the local library.

iii. A local history group may have information of use to you. The Local History Online web site **www.local-history.co.uk/Groups** is a good starting point for seeking out local history groups.

*Crossley Orphanage in Halifax was founded by three philanthropic brothers - John, Joseph and Francis Crossley*

## CHARITIES

Many children's homes and orphanages have been run by charities.

The biggest charities are in this field are Barnardos, Action for Children and the Children's Society. Between them they ran hundreds of children's homes:

### Barnardo's

Dr Barnado set up his first children's home, a ragged school in 1867 in London. Many more homes were to follow and, of course, Barnardo's still carry on work in his name today. In the very early days, the organisation was known as the *National Waifs Association*.

### Records

Barnardo's have a vast archive about the children in its care including many photographs. Apply to Barnardo's Family History Service directly and they will tell you how to apply for a search and how much it will cost.
**www.barnardos.org.uk**

*Dr Barnardo's Home for Incurable Children, Agra Mansions, Tunbridge Wells*

*National Children's Homes, Princess Alice Orphanage, Birmingham*

## Action for Children

In terms of researching the homes, you are more likely to come across Action for Children under its former name of the **National Children's Home**. The charity has been working with children for more than 140 years.

### Records

They offer a research service for family historians looking for records of individuals. However, there is a charge and, because of capacity issues, they are not always able to help. **www.actionforchildren.org.uk**

## The Children's Society

Initially known as the **Waifs and Strays Association**, it was founded in 1881 by a Church of England Sunday School teacher. By 1919, the society was running an astonishing 113 children's homes.

### Records

The Society's Records and Archive Centre has 140,000 case files chronicling the care history of every child assisted by them dating back to the Victorian period.
**www.childrenssociety.org.uk**

*The Foundation stone of the Royal Seamen's Orphanage in Portsmouth being laid in 1874 by the Duke of Edinburgh*

## TRADE GROUPS

There were some professions through which employees were becoming disabled or were even killed. It was through that some provision should be made for their children in this instance. One example of this is men who worked on the sea, another is men working on the railways. There are also at least two orphanages for the children of actors and one for the children of missionaries. With luck, the clue is in the name of the institution (and it generally is). Otherwise it is down to asking questions of archivists in the locality who might know.

On a personal basis, it is interesting to look at the census details, or death records of the parents to try and establish what did happen to the parent or parents and thus why the child entered the orphanage.

### Records

These types of benevolent organisations have diminished as health and safety in the workplace has improved. Records from the organisations, and particularly from the orphanages they ran, have not always survived. As a first step, search the Former Children's Homes website. Failing that, try the local library.

## RELIGIOUS ORGANISATIONS

Many religious organisations ran orphanages, not necessarily exclusively for children of that particular faith but that was often the case. The clue to whether a church or other institution ran a particular home is often generally in the name — Father Hudson's Homes in Coleshill, Father Berry's Homes in Liverpool. Many of the independent religious homes are Catholic in the UK, not least because it was thought that the homes runs by the Guardians of the Poor would tend to be predominantly, or in some cases exclusively, Church of England.

Some orphanages were given the name of the church which was running it.

Of course, many eighteenth and nineteenth century orphanages had a religious connection but were not necessarily run directly by the church, and many had nothing formally to do with the church. Orphanages established by the Waifs and Strays, or the National Children's Home identified as, respectively, Church of England and Methodist but were run by those organisations and not the church. Many of the philanthropists who set up orphanages did so with strong links to the church (Sir Josiah Mason set up his orphanage in Birmingham, for example, with his strong personal links to the Methodist Church), but it was the philanthropists who ran the orphanages and not the church. It is untangling the link they had with the relevant religious body that is the key to finding who to ask about records. This can often involve a bit of detective work.

### Records

In the first instance try to see if the church or other organisation associated with the orphanage still exists. For example, the local church of the same name might still be in the locality and contacting the vicar or priest might bring some invaluable information. If this does not bear fruit the steps to go through to seek out any remaining archives of religious institutions, are very similar to those as for institutions run by philanthropists.

### Catholic Orphanages

Catholic institutions are worthy of a particular mention both because of their prevalence and the complexity of tracking down records.

There has long been a tradition of Catholic organisations running orphanages - arguably this started in the Middle Ages when monasteries would take in orphans and give then religious and more general teaching. The tradition continued in the UK up to and throughout the nineteenth century. Today, it continues with local Catholic children's aid societies and many other charitable endeavours.

In the nineteenth century, there were hundreds of orphanages run by, or otherwise connected to, the Catholic Church. It is probably fair to say that finding records from these institutions is not as easy as it could be. Not only are we talking about records which are more than a hundred years old in many cases, but it is not always easy to know where to look. There is no central place of information or records. The key to finding where any surviving records might be kept is to establish precisely who ran the orphanage.

Some orphanages were run by the diocese itself. In the Roman Catholic church, a diocese is a group of parishes overseen by a bishop. The 22 dioceses of England and Wales are listed overleaf. It is possible that contacting a diocese may lead to information about an institution it once ran or which once stood within its boundaries.

Other Catholic orphanages had little or nothing to do with the diocese structure but were founded and run by particular Catholic orders. The names of some make it clear which order ran them, with others it is not so clear.

Some of the orders understood to have run orphanages:

### The Sisters of Nazareth

The Sisters of Nazareth (also known as the Poor Sisters of Nazareth), was a Catholic order founded by Victoire Larmenier (later Mother St Basil) in

# The Roman Catholic Dioceses of England and Wales

*Year established in brackets.*

## Ecclesiastical province of Birmingham

1. Archdiocese of **Birmingham** (1850)
www.birminghamdiocese.org.uk

2. **Clifton** Diocese (1850)
www.cliftondiocese.com

3. Diocese of **Shrewsbury** (1850)
www.dioceseofshrewsbury.org

## Ecclesiastical province of Cardiff

4. Archdiocese of **Cardiff** (1850)
www.rcadc.org

5. Diocese of **Menevia** (1898)
www.dioceseofmenevia.org

6. Diocese of **Wrexham** (1987)
www.wrexhamdiocese.org.uk

## Ecclesiastical province of Liverpool

7. Archdiocese of **Liverpool** (1850)
*including the Isle of Man*
www.liverpoolcatholic.org.uk

8. Diocese of **Hallam** (1980)
www.hallam-diocese.com

9. Diocese of **Hexham and Newcastle** (1850)
www.rcdhn.org.uk

10. Diocese of **Lancaster** (1924)
www.lancasterdiocese.org.uk

11. Diocese of **Leeds** (1878)
www.dioceseofleeds.org.uk

12. Diocese of **Middlesbrough** (1878)
www.middlesbrough-diocese.org.uk

13. Diocese of **Salford** (1850)
www.dioceseofsalford.org.uk

## Ecclesiastical province of Southwark

14. Archdiocese of **Southwark** (1851)
www.rcsouthwark.co.uk

15. Diocese of **Arundel and Brighton** (1965)
www.dabnet.org

16. Diocese of **Plymouth** (1850)
www.plymouth-diocese.org.uk

17. Diocese of **Portsmouth** (1882)
*including the Channel Islands*
www.portsmouthdiocese.org.uk

## Ecclesiastical province of Westminster

18. Archdiocese of **Westminster** (1622)
www.rcdow.org.uk

19. Diocese of **Brentwood** (1917)
www.dioceseofbrentwood.net

20. Diocese of **East Anglia** (1976)
www.eastangliadiocese.org.uk

21. Diocese of **Northampton** (1850)
www.northamptondiocese.org

22. Diocese of **Nottingham** (1850)
www.nottingham-diocese.org.uk

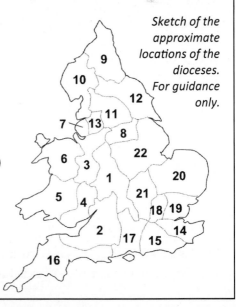

*Sketch of the approximate locations of the dioceses. For guidance only.*

1851. By 1878, there were eight homes for homeless children and poor elderly people. Other Nazareth Houses followed. As each was called Nazareth House (whether in England or abroad), this can lead to some confusion. Try to pinpoint an address before you begin your search.

The Sisters of Nazareth have an archive which does have information about some records. Any request to see records needs to be put in writing to:

Sisters of Nazareth Archive
Nazareth House
169-175 Hammersmith Road
London W6 8DB

*Nazareth House in Northampton*

**The Daughters of Charity of St Vincent De Paul**

Also known as the Sisters of Charity of St Vincent de Paul

St Vincent was a seventeenth century Catholic priest who devoted himself to working with the poor. Born in France, he founded the Daughters of Charity, Ladies of Charity and the Sisters of Charity who all worked to help people living in poverty, including destitute children. The Daughters of Charity of St Vincent de Paul established (largely in the nineteenth century) many orphanages, industrial homes, and homes for working girls in England. Many of these institutions carried the name of St Vincent. The website of the Daughters of Charity of St Vincent de Paul in the UK can be found at www.daughtersofcharity.org.uk

Incidentally, there have been numerous orders called the Daughters of Charity or the Sisters of Charity (eg. the Sisters of Charity of St Paul) and so it is important to be clear precisely which order is relevant as they are each independent of the others.

**Sisters of Mercy**

Catherine McCauley, an Irish Catholic woman, opened her first home for girls in Dublin in 1827, and founded the Sisters of Mercy in 1831. They then went on to open more homes in England, Ireland and in America. St Mary's Orphanage in Manchester and the Maryvale Orphanage in Birmingham are both recorded as having been run by the Sisters of Mercy. Their website can be found at www.sistersofmercy.org

**Brother of Charity**

Established in Belgium in 1807, the Brothers developed their work in England in 1882 and later functioned worldwide. Their patron saint is St Vincent de Paul. They ran some homes for orphans, including St Edward's Orphanage in Liverpool, for example. They have a website at www.brothersofcharity.org.uk

# STEP 4

# KNOW YOUR RIGHTS

Any organisation can hold archives. These may be in a formal setting or a cardboard box in someone's loft. Archives can be catalogued and easy to search or they may be unsorted pieces of paper. More and more often, organisations are putting lists of what they hold in archives online so people can search through them to see if there is anything that might be relevant.

What archives do have in common is that recognition that holding information about other individuals is quite some responsibility and needs to be managed accordingly. The majority of archives will have some sort of restriction about who can see their records if they contain what they consider to be 'sensitive' information.

Most archives consider any care records to be sensitive information on the basis that not everyone will want the fact that they were in care to be public information. For this reason, care records which are about individuals will generally not be available to the public. There are, however, important exceptions:

A.    If the records are about you, you have a legal right to see them (please see page 53 if you are looking for records about yourself).

B.    If the records are about a relative who has died (and you can prove that death), you may be able to see the records.

C.    The archive may decide that so much time has past since the records were made that the information can be made public. Thus, a document dated 1915 may be made public in 2015 because it has been decided that so much time has elapsed that the people who are mentioned are likely to be deceased.

However, there may still be restrictions even where the above is true:

A.    A document may be too fragile for it to be shown to the public. In this case, they might decide they have a legitimate reason to refuse to show it to you.

B.     The document may contain information which mentions other individuals. In this case, you may not be given permission to see the document.

In either of these instances, archivists might be able to copy or note down the specific element which relates to your research and let you see those even though you cannot see the whole document.

## Can the Data Protection Act help?

Many people have expressed their anger to me about the Data Protection Act and how it has hampered them in their search for information. And it is certainly frustrating to find out that a document exists which might answer all your questions and yet you are not allowed to view it.

The Data Protection Act was not established, even though it can feel like it, to annoy family history researchers. It was in fact established with little or no thought at all for archives and care records. The Act was really designed to protect the personal records that companies hold about each of us and to prevent unscrupulous companies from selling our details to other companies.

Because our details are what is considered to be personal data (information about us), as are care records, the Act has been applied to care records to help protect this sort of data (or information) from being made public.

The Act says that we have a right to know what information public bodies are holding about us as individuals. This is what gives people searching for records of their own time in children's homes the right to see their case files and other information.

Importantly, the Act also prevents information about other individuals being made public.

It is these two elements—the right of individuals to see information about themselves, and the right of individuals to have information about them kept private—that archives have to weave between.

◆     Archives generally regard care records as 'sensitive data' and thus restrict who can see them

- They may only permit the records to go public after the individual can be expected to be no longer alive

- They may charge to search the records on your behalf

- The documents themselves might be too fragile to show to the public

- Computerisation of these records is limited

## A poor fit

One of the problems with the Data Protection Act is that it is open to interpretation. As it was not specifically designed for archives and care records, archivists and the other holders of such information, have to interpret it in their own way. This leads to there being differences between different archives. While the Data Protection Act ensures that 'sensitive data' about individuals has to be treated with special care, it does not define what 'sensitive data' is in the context of children's homes. The nature of sensitive information is open to interpretation. What is also open to interpretation is how an archive should protect this sensitive data ie. who can see it. For this reason, the information you can have access to in one archive might differ from that you can see in another archive.

A common move in archives is to say that information cannot be made public if the person concerned might still be alive.

Thus, for example, some archives say that information they hold about children can be considered public after a period of 100 years and information about adults, after a period of 75 years. In this manner, they can be reassured that the data is protected during the individual's anticipated lifetime. Thus, a register for admissions which hold records about children dated 1845 to 1915 would not be considered 'open' until 2015. Other archives may interpret the guidance differently or may have different time periods in place.

These differences can be very frustrating for family history researchers who might find that they are given access to a particular document in one archive but, when they ask for the equivalent document in another archive, they are refused.

It is also possible that, outside of formal archives, information may change hands much more readily.

## Charges

The other key thing that will differ between archives is the charges that might be made. Some archivists will charge for the amount of time it takes them to find out whether any information exists about the individual you are researching and what that information might be. If you are unlucky, you might by charged a research fee to find out that no information exists.

Few care records have been digitised and so this research can take a very long time. Many admission and discharge registers are handwritten and are not in alphabetical or other useful order. Thus searching for one individual can take hours of reading. The more information you have about an individual eg. their full name and date of birth, date of admission etc. can make this process easier. However, this is often the very information we are trying to find out.

You might wonder why you cannot do through the documents yourself rather than paying an archivist do it. While you might do a great job, part of the reason archivists will often not allow you to do this is to protect any other individuals about whom the records might hold information.

## Can the Freedom of Information Act help me?

There are instances in which you might be able to use the Freedom of Information (FOI) Act to help you in your search for information. However, there are certain restrictions. The most important of these is that the Freedom of Information Act only applies to public sector organisations. Thus, the Act does not apply to records which might be held by charities, trade groups, churches and so forth. It may however, be useful in looking at children's homes which were run by the local authority.

It is always wise to check with the organisation before you make an FOI request to ensure that they won't simply give you the information without making it a formal Freedom of Information request.

An important difference between a request for information under the Freedom of Information Act rather than an informal request or one made under the Data Protection Act is that the information you request becomes public information. It is not just made available to the enquirer but is promoted publicly.

Making a formal request for information under the Freedom of Information Act is very straightforward. Simply write a letter or send an email to the organisation in question (in terms of local authorities, it might be worth making a couple of initial phone calls to see if you can track down the right department but it is not always possible).

Alternatively, the Care Leavers' Association provides a list of the appropriate departments to contact in terms of children's homes.

**http://www.careleavers.com/accesstorecords/database/**

The key information to include in your letter /email is:

♦   Your name

♦   An address where you can be contacted

♦   A description of the recorded information you want with as much detail as you can

Keep a copy of your letter or email in case you need to refer back to it or the date it was sent. The organisation then has twenty days to get in touch with you, either to give you the information you requested or to tell you when you will get it. They may charge you for photocopying but they have to let you know of this in advance.

The Freedom of Information Act, however, does not mean that you can be given information which is considered sensitive information about another individual. It does not supersede the Data Protection Act in that way. If a local authority archive has said that you cannot access information for particular genuine reasons, eg. because it is sensitive information about a third party, it is likely that the same refusal will be made to a request under the Freedom of Information Act.

The Freedom of Information Act does not apply to information which is about you. If you ask for information about yourself under the Freedom of Information Act, it will simply be dealt with under the terms of the Data Protection Act.

If you have a complaint about how an organisation has responded to your request for information, and for more information generally about both data protection and the Freedom of Information Act, contact the Information Commissioner's Office. You can call the helpline on 0303 123 1113 (see *Sources* on page 58 for more contact details).

## A few Hints and Tips

*From the enquiries I receive on the Former Children's Homes website, these are a few common pitfalls:*

**1** The names of these institutions often changed frequently through the life of the institution. Where possible, focus on the address rather than the name alone to ensure your are looking at the right place. Name changes were particularly common in 1930 when the local councils took over the Guardians of the Poor.

**2** Many institutions took in children before their formal opening date. This can mean that there is a discrepancy between the year an individual started living in the place and the official date of it opening. For example, Peter got in touch with me frustrated that he had always heard that he arrived at Edmonton Open Air School in 1937 and yet all the mentions he could find of the school stated that it didn't open until 1938. The answer could simply be that he was one of the first intake, arriving before the school was officially opened.

**3** Not all children listed in the census as being in a children's home were in care. Many staff, before the 1960s and 1970s, were residential and lived in the children's home full-time with their charges. Their own children (sometimes into their adult years) would live with them.

**4** Despite the name, not all children in orphanages were in there because they were orphans. There were all sorts of reasons, including the illness or poverty of their (living) parents, which lead to a child being placed in them. I have heard of many an occasion, for example, when a child was placed in care because Mum was about to give birth and Dad was at work and so unable to care for the family for that short time. Without research it is impossible to guess why as child might have been in care and certainly unwise to stereotype the home situations of the children in a particular home.

5 A stay in a children's home or an orphanage did not necessarily mean that a family was no longer financially responsible for their child. Some parents who placed their children in care voluntarily, say for example because they felt they could not cope but who were judged capable of making a financial contribution, had to pay a weekly fee towards the maintenance of their child.

6 During World War II, children from children's homes in cities were sometimes evacuated to safer places in the countryside. These places might be school buildings, church buildings, old large houses or the children mat have been billeted to individual family homes. Some children stayed in the areas to which they were evacuated, taking work in the local area after finishing school during the war years. Most, however, returned to the initial or another children's home in the original area. Tracing children during the war years can be tricky as there may have been many moves in what was a relatively short time.

7 The Second World War saw the development of nurseries for very young children whose mothers were working in t he war effort. Most were short-stay but some were long-stay either because of the situation of the individual family or because they became evacuation nurseries. Some of these continued as residential nurseries long after the war was over. However, not all babies were in nurseries, some were in homes with older children.

# Step 5

# 'UNOFFICIAL' RECORDS

Official records are not, fortunately, our only source of information about homes and may not be our only source of information about individuals. Perhaps when you have exhausted the official records route, you can try the unofficial records. In many cases, you will actually learn more than the records can tell you.

♦ Census

♦ Electoral roll

♦ Newspapers

♦ Getting in touch with other former residents

♦ Memories

**Census data**

Census data crosses the boundary between official and unofficial data. While it is publicly available, it also gives personal information about named individuals. The downside is, of course, that, as I write, we only have UK census data available for a 70 year period—1841 to 1911. Within the next decade, the data from 1921 will also be made available.

Many of us have come to this point through finding an ancestor on one of the census returns and discovered, through doing so that they spent some time in a childhood institution. Going back to the census return and looking at the institution as a whole means that we can find some details about the home - how many children lived there, what ages they were, how many residential staff there were and so forth. With a little patience you can build up an interesting picture of the home at the time of the census.

The census returns often refer to the children variously as inmates, pupils, scholars, orphans. All the children tend to be given the same title and it probably meant little. For example, rarely would all have been orphans.

The Irish census returns for 1901 and 1911 are available to research for free at **www.census.nationalarchives.ie**

### Electoral Roll

The electoral roll, generally accessed through the main library in any given locality, lists almigrantl the adults registered at an address in any given year This, of course, means that children, our main focus, were not listed. In some situations, it may be interesting to see how many adults were listed at the address. The roll was brought in from 1918 in the UK.

### Newspapers

Newspapers can be a fascinating source of information about children's homes. The official opening ceremony of a home many have generated a news story, for example. Events such as a sports day might also have led to a few column inches. I have even managed to find some photographs of homes and plans of their layout in old newspapers.

Newspapers can also sometimes help in researching individual children and families. A father who was killed or imprisoned resulting in his children being admitted into an orphanage, for example, might be reported in the local newspaper.

Libraries local to the children's home you are researching will no doubt have archives of old newspapers, hopefully covering the dates in which you are interested. Few of us, however, have the time or patience to go through stacks of old newspapers in the hope of happening upon a relevant story. Some archives are successfully getting newspapers online so it is always worth asking, and there is a growing UK newspaper archive online at www.nationalnewspaperarchive.gov.uk

## Getting in touch with other former residents

Some people who spent their childhoods in particular children's homes get a great deal out of being in contact with other people who were in the same home. For this reason, some people have organised groups for former residents where people can get in touch if they want to, share information and memories and perhaps even attend reunion events. These old boys' organisations can also be useful sources of information for a family historian looking to learn about what life was like in a particular home.

If there is no former residents' group for a children's home, it might be possible to get in touch with people who remember the home through a letter in the local newspaper. Some people may enjoy the opportunity to talk about their memories, others will not be so keen.

It goes with saying (but I'll say it anyway just to be on the safe side) that meeting people who spent their childhood in a home needs to be treated with sensitivity. For some, it may be an emotional experience bringing up memories and feelings which have lain dormant for some time. It is also worth remembering that not everyone's memories and experiences will be the same. I have often heard two people talking about the same home in the same era, and yet have memories which are completely different.

## Memories

Former children's homes is not a topic on which we have a great deal of preserved history. Despite the large numbers of people who have spent time in children's homes, we still know very little about these homes. And the sad fact is that we are losing, at a rapid rate, many of the people who remember these old Victorian institutions. I set up the Former Children's Homes website as a way of sharing not only the small amount of information we do have but also of supplementing our meagre resources by collecting the memories of people who lived in the homes. These preserved memories will be an important resources for the historians of the future.

Please use the site to see if there are memories there which are of interest to your own particular search, and feel free to add what you learn through your research to help those following in your footsteps.

Photographs are often rare in the life story of a child in care. Generally it is our families who take our photographs as children and our families who pay for our school photographs. A child in care might not have access to either and a photograph of themselves as a child might be something they never see. Fortunately this is something that has changed for many in the latter part of the twentieth century. Even when photographs of children's homes do exist, they have to be treated with care. Someone featuring in a group photograph, for example, may not want the knowledge that they were in a particular home to be made public.

If you come across photographs that you would like to be kept safe (they are after all precious items) and yet made accessible for those who might be in the photographs, try contacting local archives or contact the Former Children's Homes website (contact details in *Sources* page 58) for advice.

*The photographs used in this book are all 100 years old like this one of the Clacton on Sea Orphanage so that we can be sure the people featured are no longer living*

# Looking for *your own* records _____

It is a common misconception that if you spent time in a children's home you will have easy access to all your records, or you will know everything there is to know about your time there. Unfortunately, it is often the case that neither of these things is true.

There has not been a tradition of giving the young person their files or sitting down and answering their questions before they leave care. Much more care is now taken with this but this has not always been the case.

Through my work with people who spent some or all of their time in children's homes, I have heard many stories of people trying to get information about their past. Sometimes it is very straightforward information that the person wants — what children's home did I go to? When was I there? Sometimes the information being sought goes deeper — why was I put in the home? And other times the information is absolutely fundamental — do I have any family?

Many of those people talk of the frustrations about trying to access this information that is about themselves and should be their right to see.

It is the Data Protection Act which gives us our right to see any information (data) held by a public body which is specifically about us. The Act means that we can apply to see what data, say, a local authority holds about us and demand to see it. This does not necessarily mean that we get to see the original document or file, but we have a right to see the information it contains.

Thus, under the Data Protection Act, we have a right, for example, to see information held by Social Services, or the Children's Committee, and that will include information held in our case files. Asking an organisation for information they hold about ourselves is called a Subject Access Request.

For someone looking for information about themselves, the case file is the ideal source as this is likely to contain the most information. However, this is not always easy to find or to access.

# IN BRIEF

### *What you need to start the search for your records:*

**1**    **Your details**. As many details about you and the placements / homes you were in as you can remember

**2**    **The contact details** of the authority who had responsibility for your care.

- Local council / social service contact details can be found at www.careleavers.com

- The contact details of the major charities are shown on pages 32 and 33. Methods of seeking other organisations are in *Step 3* on page 31 onwards.

**3**    **ID**. You will need to prove who you are (and any name changes) with official documents (like a passport).

**4**    **Possibly some cash**. Some authorities may make a charge.

**5**    **Records.** Keep a copy of every email / letter you send and every phone call you make in your search.

**6**    **Patience**. It can take time and repeat requests before you get a response.

**7**    **Confidence** that the law is on your side. The Data Protection Act gives you the legal right to see the information that an authority holds about you..

**8**    **Luck.** Sadly you will also need luck. Now matter how hard you try, not everyone, will be given records simply because their records don't exist.

Why might you not be allowed access to your own case file:

### i. It has been destroyed

Before 1991 case files could be destroyed when the individual reached the age of 21. Many local authorities did indeed destroy case files (for records created after 1991, they must now be kept for 75 years after your 18$^{th}$ birthday).

Some case files have been destroyed accidentally. Some in, for example, flooding, others by bombing in the second world war.

### ii. It is not possible to find it

Sometimes it is simply not possible to find a case file. It can be difficult to track down individual case files especially as the children's homes or offices where they were stored have been closed.

### iii. It includes sensitive information about other people

The Data Protection Act not only gives us a right to see what information a public body holds about us, it also protects people from having their personal information shared with other people. Thus, if you and your siblings were all in care and all shared a case file, it is possible that , under the terms of the Data Protection Act , you would be refused permission to see elements of the case file which included reference to them. If you all applied to see the case file together, this might get around the problem if of course, you are in touch with your brothers and sisters. However, it may not be siblings whose information is held on the file, it could be sensitive information about other family members, the members of staff involved in your case or other children with whom you interacted. In some situations, the authority may choose simply to decline your request to see any of the information, in others, they may copy out the pieces of information relating specifically to you or give you the case file with certain elements missing (a process of concealment called 'redacting'). This can be very frustrating.

Some departments insist that you have a social worker with you when you see your case file for the first time. Others will let you take it straight home. Some local authorities will charge you for information - up to £10 to provide the information, or up to £50 for paper-based health or education records. Once you have made your request, the organisation has to respond within 40 days.

The Care Leavers' Association have done much work in this area both in terms of campaigning for people to get access to their files, and helping them request that access. They publish, on their website, details of the right departments to approach, the text of the letter to write and what to do if your request is refused.

If they draw a blank on finding your case file, it may be that you are given snippets of information from the admissions and discharge registers, or other official documents. information about yourself from other official sources, particularly the registers. If registers or minutes do exist which mention you (or might mention you). The Data Protection Act gives you the same legal right to see the information included in those documents, although not necessarily the documents themselves. The types of documents which might have records of your time in care can be found on pages 22-26.

The Freedom of Information Act does not apply to requests for information about yourself. Any such request will be treated under the terms of the Data Protection Act (see page 42 for more on this).

You may be lucky the first time you make a request for information , you may send months searching fruitlessly. You are likely to need determination and patience but never forget that it is your right - morally, ethically and legally - to see information that the authority holds about you.

# Glossary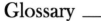

*Some of the terms you may encounter in your search*

**Accession**
The act of an item being put into an archive.

**Accommodated children**
A term introduced in 1989 to describe children in a placement that is either directly provided by the local authority or by an approved agency on behalf of the local authority.

**Admission**
The time when a child is brought into care or is admitted to a children's home.

**Archive**
A collection of historical information about an institution.

**Boarding out**
The late 19th century practice of lodging children with temporary parents, the for-runner of modern-day fostering.

**Care**
'In care' was the term describing children in the care of the local authority— the term was replaced by 'looked after' in 1989.

**Case file**
The file of papers, such as forms, reports, correspondence etc., collected and held by Social Services / Social Care relating to one individual or family.

**Children and Young Persons Act 1933**
This was a significant piece of legislation as it consolidated earlier legislation. It focused on what children could or couldn't legally do eg. it looked at children over the age of 14 not being allowed to work.

**Children Act 1948**
The UK 1948 Act was very significant in establishing the childcare service. It established Children's Department's in local councils and made it clear that it was the duty of local authorities to receive into care any child who was without parents or whose parents could not care for him for any reason.

**Closed records**
Records in an archived which are not available to the public.

**Data Protection Act**
This refers to the 1998 UK Act which applies to the processing of data on identifiable living people.

**Fostering**
Fostering is the system whereby children are placed temporarily to live with a family. In the early twentieth century the same sort of system was known as boarding out.

**Freedom of Information Act**
This is the UK Act dated 2000 which provides public access to information held by public authorities.

**Guardians of the Poor**
The individuals who sat on the Board of Guardians which ran the Poor Law Union in any given locality.

**Looked after**
Being in the care of the local authority (a term which replaced 'in care' in 1989).

**Open records**
Records in an archived which are available to the public.

**Poor Law Union**
A local government unit which existed in every locality from 1834—1930. It was run by a board of people called Guardians and had responsibility for running workhouses and children's homes associated with the workhouse.

**Records management**
The process of organising official records. It is this process which decides what records are kept, where they are kept and how long for.

**Redaction**
The act of removing words, paragraphs or pages from a file to prevent revealing sensitive information about third parties.

**Register**
A handwritten book listing admissions into the care of a particular authority or into a specific children's home.

**Repository**
The building in which an archive is kept.

**Search room**
The public room in an archive where documents will be brought to you.

**Subject Access Request**
A request for information about your self under the terms of the Data Protection Act is called a subject access request.

# Sources and resources

All these contact details were checked in October 2013. If any are incorrect, please do let us know.

**For information on former children's homes:**

www.formerchildrenshomes.org.uk

**For the National Archives:**

www.nationalarchives.gov.uk
The National Archives, Kew, Richmond, Surrey TW9 4DU
Telephone: 020 8876 3444

Scotland: The National Archives of Scotland
H M General Register House, 2 Princes Street, Edinburgh EH1 3YY
Telephone: 0131 535 1314
E-mail: enquiries@nas.gov.uk

Wales:
www.archiveswales.org.uk

**For information about accessing your own care records:**

Care Leavers' Association
www.careleavers.com
Clarendon House, 5th Floor, 81 Mosley St, Manchester M2 3LQ
Telephone: 0161 236 1980
Email: info@careleavers.com

**For information about migrated children:**

Child Migrants' Trust
www.childmigrantstrust.com
124 Musters Road, West Bridgford, Nottingham NG2 7PW
Telephone: 0115 982 2811

**For the British Newspaper Archive:**

www.britishnewspaperarchive.co.uk


**For information about workhouses:**

www.workhouses.org.uk


**For information about Data Protection and Freedom of Information Act:**

www.ico.org.uk

Information Commissioner's Office
Helpline: 0303 123 1113 or 01625 545745, 9am to 5pm, Monday to Friday

Head office: Information Commissioner's Office
Wycliffe House, Water Lane, Wilmslow, Cheshire, SK9 5AF

Northern Ireland: Information Commissioner's Office, 3rd Floor
14 Cromac Place, Belfast BT7 2JB
Telephone: 028 9027 8757 or 0303 123 1114
Email: ni@ico.org.uk

Scotland: Information Commissioner's Office
45 Melville Street, Edinburgh EH3 7HL
Telephone: 0131 244 9001
Email: scotland@ico.org.uk

Wales: Information Commissioner's Office
2nd Floor, Churchill House, Churchill Way, Cardiff CF10 2HH
Telephone: 029 2067 8400
Email: wales@ico.org.uk

# Index

# About the author

**Gudrun Limbrick** BA Hons Oxon MA Bham

Gudrun has worked as a social researcher for the last 20 years.

After completing a Masters Research and Social Policy, Gudrun became interested in oral history as a means of understanding, describing and sharing recent history. She was fortunate to work in Birmingham Archives and Heritage to create an oral history of children's homes run by the City Council. After this project, looking at more than a hundred different children's homes was completed, she realised that there was still so much more to learn and share about individual children's homes and the experiences of the people who spent all or part of their childhood living in them.

*In front of the clock tower that once stood in the middle of Erdington Cottage Homes*

She established the former children's homes website in 2011 to collect information about cottage homes throughout England and Wales and is working on a series of oral histories about children's homes.

The first of these, *The Children of the Homes: a century of Erdington Cottage Homes*, was published in 2012 and was followed quickly by other titles.

# OTHER TITLES BY THIS AUTHOR

*each based on meticulous original research*
*and the memories of people who spent their childhoods in the homes*

## The Children of the Homes
### a century of
### Erdington Cottage Homes

*"Just can't put this book down!
I've spent most of the day reading -
I should be doing the decorating..."*

ISBN: 978-1-903210-28-4

---

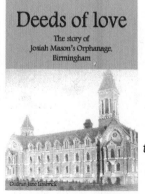

## Deeds of Love
### The Story of Josiah Mason's Orphanage
### in Birmingham

*This orphanage was started by the industrialist, Sir
Josiah Mason, as an act of charity. The enormous
building was demolished in the 1960s leaving little
trace of the hundreds of children who once lived there.*

ISBN: 978-1-903210-24-6

---

## The Homes on the Hill
### The story of Cosham Cottage Homes,
### Portsmouth

*The cottage homes were opened in 1930 and remained
open for only 30 years. Despite their short existence,
they have witnessed terrible controversy.*

ISBN: 978-1-903210-22-2

## ORDER FORM OVERLEAF

| No. of copies | Title | Price per copy |
|---|---|---|
| | *The Children of the Homes: a century of Erdington Cottage Homes* | £12.99 |
| | *Deeds of Love: The story of Josiah Mason's Orphanage* | £12.99 |
| | *The Homes on the Hill: the story of Cosham Cottage Homes* | £11.99 |
| | *How to research childhoods spent in former children's homes* | £8.99 |

NAME: ...........................................................................................................

ADDRESS: .....................................................................................................

.....................................................................................................................

.....................................................................................................................

...............................................................POSTCODE: ..................................

EMAIL: .........................................................................................................

*Please add £1.60 for the first copy and 90p per copy for each additional copy towards postage and packing (UK only).*

**Total enclosed: £ ...................................**

Please make cheques payable to **WordWorks** and send, with order to:
**WORDWORKS, 120 SCHOOL RD, MOSELEY, BIRMINGHAM B13 9TS**

## YOU CAN ALSO ORDER THEM THROUGH...

# www.formerchildrenshomes.org.uk

amazon.co.uk        ebay